SAFETY FIRST

Bike Safety

by Kirsten Chang

BLASTOFF! READERS 1

BLASTOFF! READERS, AN IMPRINT OF BELLWETHER MEDIA BY FLUTTERBEE

Blastoff! Readers are carefully developed by literacy experts to build reading stamina and move students toward fluency by combining standards-based content with developmentally appropriate text.

Level 1 provides the most support through repetition of high-frequency words, light text, predictable sentence patterns, and strong visual support.

Level 2 offers early readers a bit more challenge through varied sentences, increased text load, and text-supportive special features.

Level 3 advances early-fluent readers toward fluency through increased text load, less reliance on photos, advancing concepts, longer sentences, and more complex special features.

★ **Blastoff! Universe**

This edition first published in 2027 by Bellwether Media, Inc.

For information regarding permission, write to Bellwether Media, Inc., Attention: Permissions Department, 3500 American Blvd W, Suite 150, Bloomington, MN 55431.

Library of Congress Cataloging-in-Publication Data is available at www.loc.gov or upon request from the publisher.

ISBN: 9798898800345 (hardcover)
ISBN: 9798898802875 (paperback)
ISBN: 9798898801588 (ebook)

Editor: Rachael Barnes Designer: Andrea Schneider

Printed in the United States of America, North Mankato, MN.

Table of Contents

Safety First

Milo learns to
ride his bike.
He wears a helmet.
He stays safe!

helmet

Why Stay Safe?

Riding bikes is fun! We pedal hard and go fast. But **accidents** can happen.

accident

Bikes can **skid** when they hit big bumps. Falls can hurt!

skidding

Rules for riding bikes help **protect** us and the people around us.

Staying Safe

Tim wears a helmet
that fits just right.
It protects his head.

Rory's bike is the right size. She checks the tires, brakes, and **chain**.

chain
tire

Link wears sneakers.
It is safer to pedal!

pedaling

Anna and Luis ride on sidewalks. They stop at stop signs. They use hand signals.

How Hand Signals Work

Ian and Mom wear **reflective** clothes. They have a fun evening bike ride!

Safety Rules

- Choose a **helmet** and **bike** that are the right size.
- Check the bike's **tires**, **brakes**, and **chain**.
- Wear **safe shoes** and **reflective clothes**.
- Stop at **stop signs**.

Glossary

accidents

sudden events when someone is hurt

chain

a loop on a bike that moves power from the pedals to the wheels

protect

to keep safe

reflective

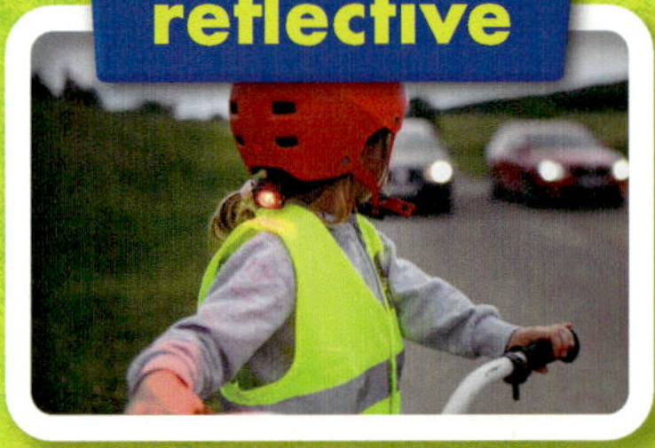

able to bounce light off its surface

skid

to slide without turning

To Learn More

AT THE LIBRARY

Bassier, Emma. *Bike Safety*. Minneapolis, Minn.: Pop!, 2021.

Catena, Melissa. *Bike Safety*. Minneapolis, Minn.: Jump!, 2025.

Chang, Kirsten. *Street Safety*. Minneapolis, Minn.: Bellwether Media, 2027.

ON THE WEB

FACTSURFER

Factsurfer.com gives you a safe, fun way to find more information.

1. Go to www.factsurfer.com.
2. Enter "bike safety" into the search box and click 🔍.
3. Select your book cover to see a list of related content.

Index

The images in this book are reproduced through the courtesy of: Volodymyr, front cover (top), pp. 4-5; Satjawat, front cover (bottom); SURF3D, p. 3 (tire); PNGLovers, p. 3 (helmet); torwaiphoto, pp. 6-7, 16-17; Ermolaeva Olga, p. 7 (inset); nazar_ab, pp. 8-9, 22 (skid); Sergey Novikov, pp. 10-11; MARIA GARCIA, pp. 12-13; MSTORY, pp. 14-15; Fly View Productions, pp. 18-19; Jecapix, pp. 20-21; Ermolaev Alexandr, p. 22 (accidents); Alexander, p. 22 (chain); evgenyatamanenko, p. 22 (protect); Halfpoint, p. 22 (reflective); vectorfusionart, p. 23.